THE MIRACULOUS,
SOMETIMES

THE MIRACULOUS,
SOMETIMES

Meg
SHEVENOCK

CONDUIT BOOKS
& EPHEMERA

Rainer Maria Rilke hesitates whether to abandon a bar of soap in a hotel room. During Gilles de Rais' confession, the Bishop of Nantes covers the cross....If a cross is a witness, why not a loaf of bread, or a shoe-tree, or a sugar-tongs, or a piece of string?

—Dennis Silk, "The Marionette Theater"

ISBN: 978-1-7336020-3-7

Published by Conduit Books & Ephemera
788 Osceola Avenue, Saint Paul, Minnesota 55105
www.conduit.org

Book design by Scott Bruno/b graphic design

Distributed by Small Press Distribution
www.spdbooks.org

Cover photo courtesy the Library of Congress.
Carol M. Highsmith, "Abandoned house near Granville, Vermont," 2017.

CONTENTS

THE
DARK
LINE

Of the Man Who Touched Me

at seventeen, in a hot tub, *oh, cliché,*
but wait, there's a part I never say—
his wife was in it, too. And she and I wore
his boxers for bathing suits, and the long
gentle pines towered over us,
and the sharp little stars were out, too far
to make a call, so well we were removed
from the rest of the world. And each of us,
in our own brains, pretended
all was usual, nothing *un-*
about this bath, nothing not
ok, not when I lifted my dripping body,
see through in white, for cool,
not when he navigated froth
to stick his big toe through my hot little hole.
Not moans formed our mouths,
but words, casually sweating above the surface,
though a careful ear would've caught the crumple
in my vocal cords, the lilt inside his *relaxing—*
such masquerade—his wife's mourning flowers,
withered in their winter beds. I rested my head
against the marbled rim. Trained my mind
on the dark. I wore this position
Monday, back in his class at school.
All of it is true.

"Everything that does not need you is real"

One solution is: somewhere,
there's a child who doesn't need me,
so she'll never be born.

I sass the fact,
talk back: *what do* I *need?*

Wildness. Raw scenes. A seagull
pecks a live crab on the beach,
tearing golden threads from its plated gut.
Eat it, I think. *Eat its fucking guts out.*
The crab's claws pant in the air, so terrible
I can't look away.

From there, all I can see
are bits of garbage in the weed:
shoelace, Styrofoam, rusted ring.
And all the plastic rainbow of things
battered to debris.

I walk and photograph
the smallest of these—
I can't stop. It is so ugly.

I want to tie things up.

Because his eyes traced my body, disrupting the vast cold swaths.

Because I learned to move knowing my movement would be memorized, my gestures, weighted: pulling out a chair, taking a sip, lifting a strip of film up to the light.

Because, *of x, y—that without it, I would never—*

voice, the quality of graphite, when fingers grip a pencil so hard, it indents the table beneath the dark line, as though dividing *here* from not being. On the surface, a visible *seems to be saying,* but secretly, underneath it, the felt thing. I trace my finger over and over the groove, feeling everything I'm not saying, while relying on descriptions of sadness, like what it means to be saved by a balloon's sun-bleached string.

ORDER

OF

DEBRIS

Debris, from early eighteenth century: from French *débris*, from obsolete *débriser* to break down.

Flu season, sliding in and out of consciousness, a loud voice enters through a corner of upper-blue, *Is that why we watch TV?,* when I think about the reliability of my death, of all our deaths.

In defiance, turn to almost anything—tree roots, chain-link, hard sun on quarry walls—Sundays, summers ago—trespassing to leap into perfectly clear water, massive, black rocks below.

The feeling of nothingness above massive, black rocks.

Or not quite *nothing,* but the vast cold swaths of not being held, blind limbs kicking or, sinking, as I floated, face only above the surface, like a flung mask. It's a feeling I carry. I can go either way.

When [desperate], *Exhibit A:* plastic shopping bag trapped in the branches of a tree, inflates and deflates with every gust. Lung of the universe, in pure garbage.

The miraculous, sometimes.

The first abandoned house I loved I glimpsed through trees. From the school bus, fleeting snapshot of its sagging porch and crooked shingles. Immediately, I made it mine on the premise, *nobody else cares.* Fifteen, lonely, starting to accept my own strangeness—I couldn't not care about it.

The next day, I got off the bus early, and walked through the trees toward the house. Pushed open the rusted screen. Cobwebs in the cross-hatch, thick as faint down.

That first time there was a feeling inside which never failed to cease, of someone, or something, waiting. Not so much in a horror movie sense, although my skin tightened in the late October heat—but a sense of waiting without anyone or anything to wait for, slow crumble of time, a waiting of my own invention, i.e., time which waits for nothing, no one.

I opened every drawer in the new house. Candles, envelopes in ballpoint, disintegrating, lace-edged slips. Mice, curled like commas. It mattered, these things: melted, crackled, stained, remained.

When something matters, it means something, or to mean something is to matter. Is this not how every narrative begins?

Or, it begins from an empty space inside the body, loosely floating among the organs, longing to become taut, full of matter; it's its failure that feeds.

Each visit to the house made my narrative more precise, like beads passed along a needle, threading me to the moment at the kitchen sink, my body blurred into a girl on any day, doing the dishes, even as soot blackened the porcelain basin. An eye on the field behind, waiting for someone to come in with the dusk, light winnowing like a hood pulled shut. Uncomfortably electric to think: how many cups and saucers had passed under the running water, where water no longer ran, where once, there was no reason to imagine the water no longer running?

Lips chapped, dry column of air. A teacup cracked fine as a hair.

From a striped-pink mattress at the top of the attic stairs, I looked down to the second-story landing, where a window framed a view of solid leaves. Heady, green, archetype of the world that was: possibility. Bright, overwhelming fullness. Fullness beside the rot, the sill dotted with dead bees.

I would fashion my existence of debris. High-heels, slip-ons, oxfords, wing-tips. The lovely eyelets. Soles worn in places, so exact. Looking at them, my heart glowed cartoonish. Velvet hangers with nothing to wear! The everyday of getting dressed, a mind to the fabric, never the moths.

I tried something half-gone on. An eaten lace across my collar. I was the future. Or the past. Heartbeat, the present.

Like the early experiments of childhood: if I touch the wood in this exact place, and say to myself, *Remember this moment, for the rest of your life,* will I remember this moment for the rest of my life?

The place I touched has turned to dust. I drew a diamond in the dust, and then a chain of diamonds. I stopped when the dust ran out.

I remember where it stopped.

How many days did the sun go down like a bloody yolk, or clouded descend behind a navy rag, wrung, stretched across an open line, while I sat on the stoop stroking blades of grass, my eyes and throat illumined with veins, and leaned forward into the blood, for which the word, *coursing,* a word suggesting wildness but also fear, bears with it, by association, *alive*?

Questions like this, I was obsessed, refused simple, cried when I couldn't paint the box entirely black, enough to mean no stars, that we can see, so how can that mean everything, submit "everything," when everyone knows it isn't, but says it is, so we can just, can't we just, *move on please,* dumb cardboard, believe?

That first time there was a feeling inside which never failed to cease, of ~~someone, or~~ something ~~waiting~~ *happened to* someone-not-me. Not so much in a horror movie sense, although my skin tightened ~~in the late October heat~~ when he touched me. But a sense of waiting ~~without anyone or anything to wait for, slow crumble of time maybe, a waiting of my own invention, i.e., *time* which waits for nothing, no one,~~ to be annihilated.

An apple with my teeth marks kept one full year under my bed, young, surely I didn't already know how to let, go on, dream of worms the same color as what they swallowed, when I pulled the bag back through dust, insides moved,

When something matters it means something, or to mean something is to matter.

This part's a narrative too, although it's easier to talk about a cloth-bodied doll with lolling head and pink, heart-shaped lips, and how I found her floating in a pile of ancient newspapers, sparkle-eyed, searching for the sky, where instead, flaking plaster, and a bird's nest dangled from the ceiling.

Imagine that the doll and the bird were friends, maintaining a half-animate company as the newspapers drifted increasingly farther from the day, and nobody ever returned.

Just as the past drifted and the doll in the newspapers remained, the man gradually stood closer and closer to me, until, one afternoon, as casually as you would reach out to open a door, he touched me.

I mean enough on a crystal tour of Echo Caverns, deep inside a cold trail, strangers make a human rail, single-file no flash is how to practice, soft jokes, *stalact-, stalagm-,* invisible hair between, minerals dripping eternities, to almost always meet, *I want to see a crystal* how about, I turn the lights out, our own hands, before our faces, *ready set* I got to, flick the switch, plunge us, one minute into, we couldn't tell if our hands were, there, or the degree to which, I was trying, to paint the shoebox, about the absence

Always, the center seat, biting my cheek,
quiet in his class at school.

I didn't ask for help.

But as I struggled to maneuver the film
into the canister, his hand met mine
in the dark of the nylon changing bag.

In the beginning, it was my hand or my shoulder, a squeeze and a lingering, a little too long. In truth, I wanted to cry onto his chest, darken the cotton, there in the empty hallway under the raw fluorescent lights. A few broken pencils on the floor. Beneath strains of muffled lecturing. I grew weak where his hand was, a child. When I think about it now, ~~I don't think it's my fault~~ I want to throw up.

At some point drinking from a hose—for a long time this image alone, then
a voice, "are you entering the room nobody knows?" When I'd look back
through fake flowers, ruffling their silk for something else, a scent, a sign,
piano past sadness I never practiced, what was my art at age x, library books
I guess, lines impressed, "nobody knows," or called to stage directly, before
the microphone, *I don't know why I wish I could stay,* a loose golden alone,
sometimes simply "not there," run, through the forest, and feel, the fullness
of, breathing

Things magnified. Body, mind. Magnified, the tiny white and sepia images. on film. In the abandoned house, I photographed myself with crescents of glass against my skin. In the crumpled image I still possess, snow is visible through the broken window. In the moment, I could not feel the whitened tips of my fingers, adjusting for light. I set the timer and crawled through the ship-wreck scene of the eight-degree room, to take my place beside the low window. I cradled the glass delicately, testing its sharpness against the taut undersides of my breasts.

I would hide the image in the drying rack, bottom shelf or pushed to the back. Later on, alone in the room, he would poke around and find me there.

As the teacher, it was his right to look at his students' work. Was it also his responsibility to say, "No more nudity"? Instead, he brought me books by photographers whose subjects were mostly nude, mostly women. Sitting beside me to discuss a print, he used the word, "voyeuristic." Floating a finger above my thigh, he said, "The angle, it's perfect." If questioned, surely, he would have played the art card. But his cock was hard. Did I know these things? I think I knew them, but it felt impossible, terrifying.

Fragments, for my mind to feel past, as a child, coloring the slope of the Mariana Trench, an arrow points to this last part that has a name, meaning we think we know it, like we know we don't, for what comes after, liquid sound, brightest blind fish, nothing's ever an outline to begin with, but the hidden, heart of cells

I continued to photograph myself in the house, or sometimes, in my family's cinderblock basement, among the plastic toys and novelty liquor bottles, beneath the sounds of my parents fighting, sisters fighting, dog barking, someone throwing cereal and keys and magazines across the room. I rubbed dirt or mold or cobwebs onto my face or chest or thighs. I didn't know why, exactly, these self-portraits treading decay, though I followed a conscious thread connecting my heart to the earth. What it means to *be*—in the moment, as when the shutter released—and later, to *be* outside it, and later, much later, though not necessarily much, to not at all be.

While the process was euphoric, in every image my expression is overwhelmingly distant or sad. Looking at them, he wanted to put his fingers inside me, his mouth on my breast, my hand on his cock (and did, and did, and did).

Quietly the fields' ungreening, then every summer came, I would start
to panic, how to get through each day, dissolved, massively blank, this
sad experiment gum wad, collected more dust, I set it on the gold lamp,
"living" sculpture and still, in glasses, with giant questions, every corridor
of the television was too loud, but once we found kittens in a barn where
my mother made love, rainbows later from a crystal swam the humidity
of the room, sometimes skimming the animals so fast, feeling the colors'
translucence, I am not, made of bones

Beside the chemicals in the darkroom. Past the late bell in the stairwell.
In the parking lot, in his pickup, in a snowstorm.

Etc., until:

under the rafters of a barn. At the edge of a forest. On the lip of a pitch-
black lake.

Etc., until, eventually:

in a hot tub under the stars. In a dingy hotel room. With his camera
peepholed before his eye, and an open beer I refused in fear, sweating on
the bedpost, and me, poised on the ratty rug in my pattern of rosebuds
underwear, paid for by my mother.

Slave to the disgust, I have to turn away now for something else, say, cutting out birds the size of punctuation, and gluing them to the pages of a nineteenth century photo album, whose every window for a photograph is empty, so that a literal corridor extends through the middle of the book. It seems something holy could happen inside there. Nothing preordained. A secret arbor to disappear in, beneath a flock of darkling birds.

I was a minor; I was underage; I was "a mature 15"; "a mature 17"; I was "beyond the emotions of her peers"; I was guilty; I was worried about my parents' divorce; about my sisters' sadness; that we had no money; that we were going to live on the street; I quit sports; I let the strange come out; I soaked my photographs in peroxide; I breathed the fumes ecstatically; I set a fire in my room; I skipped school; I did my homework; I listened top-notch to Kate Bush braying like a donkey; I loved feral heroines; I masturbated all the time; I fasted until my ribs showed; I ran by the creek at night; I hammered my cheekbone quietly; I stripped in the cemetery so he could draw me; I went by his house afterschool; I went when his children were out; I went when his wife was working; I spent the weekends lying; I spent the evenings writing poems; I was easy prey; I ate an orange a day; I peeled it slowly; I prepared to die.

But I remember how, once, he left a silver dollar on the hotel pillow for me to find when I woke.

Once, on a fire escape, I smoked weed with his son who was closer to my age, and who I thought would never go for me, and didn't, because, as he explained it, he was too old for me.

And once, I did finally drink a beer, my first beer, in a bar with him, in the middle of nowhere, on a Saturday night, the tables packed with bikers and loud male voices, and halfway through the bottle my body began streaming out of me in slowly dissolving particles, my body leaving my body, and suddenly I had a moment of clarity, as I sometimes still do following a drink, of *Oh, shit. Oh, shit.*

I have to continue to turn away, taking comfort in arrangements, inventing order where previously I felt none. Three iridescent fragments from a tide pool, in a black, velvet-lined box, whose satin rafter says TIMES—not TIME, but TIMES. I don't know the origin or intention of the box, but each fragment, as I line it on the velvet, is smaller than my fingernail, having emerged from the ocean into salty pools among the sharp rocks, where, by chance, my eyes aligned with their unconscious shine.

Surely it's a shining I stole, selfish for some beauty that I could claim, by placing it in this box.

Though who am I to say what's conscious and what's not? Might I be as conscious as a fragment, all my tumbling distilled to silence. Might the fragments have preferred to remain in the shallows of the sea. Nobody asked them what they wanted, assuming they would not speak.

GARBAGE
MIRACLES

In the bushes, I find a lavender piece of leather puckered by a red snap. The leather's rectangularly shaped, a loose swatch whose stitches, also red, reveal their slow dissolve. Weather has stained a dark line down the lavender. The assemblage speaks to me. Object and affect. At home, I glue plant roots across its surface, tending the delicate mass. Culling these disparate lives to order, where previously I felt none, is a way toward memory: knocking earth from the nodules is combing knots from a young girl's hair.

In Dickinson's "Banish Air from Air—" she uses parlance of the day to call lace "blond." Fabrics named for hair, or hair named for fabrics. Hair ultimately is compared to the plants from which the fabrics grew, or to the fur and bones of other animals. Flax, ebony, ivory. I see bread, horses, a jungle. These solids born in color as in sound, allocate the air, like a prism serves us back same light transformed. I relate to whatever in the room belies emptiness: clear made color, dust that used to be flowers. Something always there implies a level of safety, though I also close my fingers around a living branch, so much more certain when the world's edges seem to frail.

Jamie and I make a sculpture with erasers, four of them floating in the middle of the wall. The erasers are classic pink, smudged with the evidence of mistakes, except one is blue and says ERASER in large letters, proclaiming of itself the thing that will in time, devour its proclamation. I do not know what to call this. The snake that swallows its own tail, suggests, eventually, we won't be able to discern a beginning. Fights back, from a shelf a few paces down, a sculpture Jamie made: generic floss dispenser whose original text is worn almost completely, over which Jamie has written:

IF I CAN'T EVEN FINISH A TUBE OF TOOTHPASTE,
HOW WILL I EVER LEARN TO DIE?

I have records I can only listen to only when Stephen's not home. They're a thick swim through sorrow and I love, for a little while, to be full of sorrow, reaching from my place on the floor to replace the needle in the same groove repeatedly, pressing the bruise, while the sky drains to dark. I go out of my way to obtain handkerchiefs whose aesthetic I can appreciate when I sob, sitting on the couch on a Sunday, with picnic sounds drifting over the fence in the kind of scenario that makes me cry harder. People who seem absolutely fine and who know how to enjoy a good day say, "Please pass the salt." Charcoal implies lightheartedness. These kinds of etceteras. The novelist Hanya Yanagihara said, speaking about her devastating novel *A Little Life,* that she "wanted to make a character that started here"—drawing a low dot in the air, then squiggling a line of a life before returning to the same low dot—"and ended here." Psychologists wrote her angry letters against this presumption that some people "can't get better." Yanagihara held her ground: "Many people can, but some people can't. We live in a culture that does not want to accept this." I don't believe about myself that I need to get better, or can't get better, but I believe sadness is part of who I am, and sometimes, I have to nurse from it.

Robin suggested my "fear of having a body" as my subject I can't escape. Several weeks later I realized that animals are my god, a shock that descends through me like an anchor when our dog, Coda, stretched on bricks in the sun, blinks, and raises her twitching nose in the air, clearly fulfilling whatever she is meant to, here to be and do exactly as she appears before me.

To face the curtain falling feeling before sleep, my therapist says to "make an appointment with my anxiety," which means somewhere besides my bed, before going to bed, address this. I choose the couch for the addressing of death. My couch that is covered in dog hairs, ink stains, body impressions. Sitting up formally, with my hands prayer-like I try to go straight into the nothingness. As a child, I concentrated on my teeth in the mirror, thinking at my image, *Someday that will be the last of you.* Tap-tap, fingernail on tooth. I knew then as now, the tapping meant there was a brain to think about it, a heart to slam about it, and later there would be neither brain, nor heart. I started to look for miracles.

One of the greatest of these instances involves marbles, two marbles that I found in the past decade, half-submerged in the dirt of two different forests, two different years, well off the path of common tread and clear of any visible ruins. Two marbles in the woods. One is porcelain-white, eye without iris. One is solid periwinkle, color of floating. They make a lovely pair: the unseeing eye floats through the spacelessness of the other. The white marble was a surprise but less shocking than when I found its partner, years later. The periwinkle marble was hardly showing through dirt beneath a crop of mountain laurel. I was hiking and I happened to look down or I looked down because I was meant to, or the stars aligned to make me look down, or God pushed my head toward the ground, and there I saw a speck of beautiful cream-purple. I used a small rock to dig the marble out.

This moment mimicked other intimate moments with the earth that I keep going back to, digging and scraping to find the pieces I need to build a monumental belief. I want a belief to fight against what goes, as in the first time lovesick in my adult life, traipsing through a nearby schoolyard on a cold April Saturday, I saw a sequin on the surface and bent over. When I pulled it, earth pulled. I know why I choked—a string of sequins after months of being buried. In my life while the sequins waited, the person I loved left me; I felt the thaw, but slow, like a mouthful of snow.

In the mirror, focus on the teeth, touch the sockets, smooth the skull where the eyes click: mask, I will eventually back out of.

I spent a hundred hours or more on the couch of my molester, waiting for him to wake. This couch was where I began my obsession with earth, as in, *dirt*. It was always under my fingernails; it was also not far under me, under the floor. I often went to bed without a shower, on humid days, lying there in a coat of filth too fine to see. When I could hear him breathing, I crept outside to pee in the grass after holding it for so long. It was so completely dark. It was so absolutely quiet. I held my knees and rocked in the cold grass while the heat streamed out of me.

The grass was a cold, kind thing when I crouched in it, rocking slowly, myself dissolved like a tablet in dark water.

"A child said *What is the grass?* fetching it to me with full hands;
How could I answer the child?"

Impossible, sobbing. My molecules among the pines.

Even now I try to protect those who I might prosecute by not speaking out. I say *what's past is past* while dragging the past behind me like a body. I care about the chance of ruining lives more than I take care of my own life, and yet how can I know how peacefully they carry on: his wife, his once young son.

When my father got laid off, my mother, by way of explaining what it *meant,* said, "It *means* we will get holes in our underwear and the elastic will stretch out and we will not be able to replace them." I put my face down on the greasy table and cried. Since then I always try to keep decent underwear and also make them last for a long time, and even after they're done lasting, I still don't throw them away.

I wanted to be fed. I was so thin and ate only when someone wanted to feed me, like a domestic animal. He would go on vacation with his family, and I would eat the apple in his backyard, masturbating on the picnic bench under a wide white sky.

This morning I called a flock of circling doves *doves* until, it turned out, they were vultures. How stupid. Every bird, not *birds,* and yet silhouetted in sky they are all weightless, own their element thoughtlessly through hollowed bone, altitude, the languageless gliding. Without god, I need the birds to get me out of bed in the morning. But white noise helps me fall asleep; as soon as I wake I turn off the white noise and get back into bed so I can hear the birds.

His hands were elegant like a surgeon's or boxy like a construction worker's. A lot of it simply doesn't matter.

He had nice nails. Confident.

He didn't send me text messages because they were hardly invented, and I was a youthful girl without a personal phone, which is to say, this kind of thing has been happening forever, which is to say, grown men, hurdling work, families, the law, still find ways to get girls with their Levi's unzipped inside their cars, in a snowstorm.

Nature made everything for a minute seem so soft. The windshield completely buried. His finger jerked inside me while all around in the abandoned parking lot, the world seemed to beautifully end. I looked at the snow and the end. I fell in love with them.

At home my father packed his belongings in tiny busted duffel bags, raising every item in front of his face to shout some goddamns. My mother in bed watching black and white TV, turned the volume up.

Stoicism was a posture I designed to keep the peace. Don't move, don't speak and you can go on inside your own head, searching for exits to dreamy things. This prepares you with strategies for later pain. As far as I could see it, my parents didn't love each other; it's not their fault. I like to believe they tried.

I assume I am "apart" from emergency in my body when I am not actually being treated. But in the animal ER, while Coda is treated for intestinal distress, I absorb the pain of each animal as it comes through the door: the tiny terrier hit by a car, shaking in a woman's arms while her children hold the counter and sob; the greyhound with shockingly pink puncture wounds; the enormously fat yellow lab panting by the door; the cat grimly quiet in its carrier. Several times I tear up and have to face the wall, while we wait for Coda to be returned to us. The looks on peoples' faces are the same as the looks worn by passengers in the human ER, everyone hoping that this time, it won't be the last news, hoping we can keep on denying the inevitably of last news for a lot longer. Safe for now. Coda comes bounding out as if nothing at all is wrong and thankfully, nothing is, save some nervous reaction for which we have not yet found a common language.

But what of that man who has made the chopped tips of orange and yellow school pencils look to me like violence? That man who in turn led me to other men who made the chopped orange and yellow pencil tips look like even more violence? What of that man who has soured, by association, the only tool I remotely know what to do with? I will tell you: he breathes easily.

But I love these pencil bits. I Scotch-tape them to sticks in crude approximation of possible/impossible. Then, after feeling them stupid for several weeks, one day, holding one up against the dirty basement carpet in the sun, I decide it's one of the best things I've ever made.

When the dentist leans his stomach into the top of my head with his hand in my mouth, I think, *This is too much for an ordinary moment,* and if I had to characterize the feeling I would say it is "no big deal" and gentle and terrible at the same time. This too, is what life is—a not overly soft, grown man stranger's stomach just barely pressing the top of my skull as I hang upside down with my eyes shut, and wait for the scene to be over, and afterwards, we won't even exchange a look that acknowledges it though, "When your bill arrives you might note that I gave you a discount," my dentist says, on my way out the door.

Tap-tap.

Obsessed with the five second flashback in Buñuel's *Belle de Jour* in which the main character, Severine, who has serious intimacy problems, is pictured as a child standing helplessly in a domestic foyer, while a man reaches his hand up her wool skirt, and she leans back rigidly like a bundle of sticks. Several critics, including Roger Ebert, failed to mention this crucial aspect of Severine's past when dissecting how and why she might refuse her handsome, rich, loving husband and simultaneously prostitute herself to a bunch of masochists. Ebert, writing about Severine's character, quoted Woody Allen, of all people, who said, "The heart wants what the heart wants," defending his relationship with his stepdaughter. Allen is in fact, and without acknowledgement, quoting Emily Dickinson, who wrote, in a letter to a grieving friend, 1862:

"When the Best is gone—I know that other things are not of consequence—
The Heart wants what it wants—or else it does not care"

Where are my garbage miracles on a toneless, weatherless day? Sometimes I get by on a scrap of yellow paper, blowing like another lifetime down the street. Or the loose thread quivering cursive from the loquat tree. It wants to finish what it has to say. I respect that it stays silent, just as I implore it. When my heart is heavy I pay more attention to what we call the trash.

And sometimes, when my spirit gets really down, I walk Coda up the hill like we have forever to do this; climbing slowly, this morning around six, I noticed the moon half there in the already blue sky, and I wished it was chalk someone had gently smudged across my cheek, and then I could hardly feel the touch of the moon on my face, and I began to cry.

Several hours later, reclining on the servicing table, my acupuncturist touched my cheek in the exact spot and said, "What is this mark here—a crease from your pillow?" I had been awake by then for hours.

My heart goes out of my body for a second when I pick up off of the street the bleached balloon string with the nub end of a pink balloon. Now it is hung on the wall, attached to a clipboard with a faded photograph of the sun. These things too, were meant to be together. I think about the balloon's life every time I pass.

And when I walk Coda, sometimes I deliberately bump my leg into her side, just to feel the living.

Years later, once or twice he pulled over on the side of the road to call me, hopeful. On break from college, I took the calls in my divorced mother's country backyard and, in full nonchalance, pacing barefoot in the grass, I detailed how I was sleeping with someone my own age, someone so exciting, available, *a real artist.* He sounded sad while trying to sound happy. "I miss you," he said, and "maybe someday…"

Shh, there are deer coming out of the forest to lick the salt!

From the kitchen window of my mother's new rental, I loved that salt lick's shine in an ocean of green June. Dense, glistening, oddly knobbed, an unreal white against the landscape. I walked out periodically to touch the melting, awed by the geometric mass that constantly remained, despite hours the deer spent there with their uncannily human tongues, devouring.

A long pen and ink mouth moves against the sunset, thins into river and twists through root and rock before finding its shape on the other side of the mountain, blossoming into flower, ripe though changed, to speak in the same voice, the same.

Or elsewhere, temporality: sunset, an ink-lined mouth.

And again, as I'm trying to say, as Ann puts these things, "what aches to look at":

> *I pulled the tablecloth over my shoulders*
> *he leaned into a painting*
> *and that was it*
> *for summer*

What you won't go back to, can't go back to, can't return to your childhood bedroom after all, to find the animal sheets still warm from your Saturday morning body. Someone downstairs opens the screen to collect the newspaper. The date has dissolved, and what you dreamed—

Writing with a white pencil on a white piece of paper, or with a blue pencil on a blue piece of paper, or with a black pencil on a black piece of paper, I feel more than I would if I could see what I had written there.

I wrap each of my fingers in tissue paper and suck them, until, thoroughly wet, I can shape and slip free the almost disintegrating forms. Loose, yet holding, I set them on the kitchen table to dry. They look like the see-through ghost necks of horses. Ghosts of my fingers frozen, mid-sprint, with knucklebones for heads.

I make hundreds and present them as *really not that interesting to anyone else* or *I don't know what this is other than hours of sucking.* I cannot let them go. In time I realize that the "not being able to let them go" is the piece.

Some afternoons hanging over the keyboard, pretending I feel something enough to say it. It is hard to ignore the squiggly red and green suggesting *you really don't mean—*? But yes. No, and yes. I would like to get away from the machine. I would like to get some real erasers, hundreds and hundreds of the classic pink erasers prized by young girls on the first day of school, prized so much they kiss their clean, error-free erasers that are the same color as the insides of their kissing mouths. But I would like the erasers after many shameful errors have been made, after the girls have worn holes through their math and grammar worksheets, have littered their desks with hot pink rubber pills and graphite streaks that saliva only intensifies into stormy gray spit clouds on the tops of their desks. Here, I remember what it's like, here, where it smells like bodily fluids, and burning rubber and shame.

THAT
WAS
THEN

Growing up, my mother washed all our things in scent-free detergent, whose absence of smell overwhelmed me with its definite *thereness,* a faint nothing odor of something, undeniable, when, head muffled deep in the linen closet, I reached for a faded flower sheet, and sometimes fell in love so well with comfort, I rested there a moment, in the grains of dark,

my body, swallowed, in the house behind.

That was then. Yet, since a teenager, I have defined the day by what I make or not, and does it undo me madly all alone like I want it to, so to break the surface of speech, afterwards, is nearly impossible, like, just try this basic exchange with the cashier about bananas, who wonders if he should help you to the car, based on your—only a parcel—

you can manage on your own, you weren't molested for nothing,

not to be abrupt, but

your body is more than capable of bearing.

And now you want a baby. Not all bodies can have what they want. Some bodies thrash in their own dark lakes, imagining their organs on a cottage shelf, like in tenderness, to be haunted, not *I love you,* but *you are mist*— as in *missing,* touch your gut when waking, touch your breast when, after dreams of nursing the dog, for smears of months unfailing, these empty mornings, when the blood comes.

Not embarrassed that I nursed my dog in a dream, but that I have failed to
make a baby, after saying how much I wanted one. Like I said to the cashier,
Thank you, but I can take care of
       myself.

Retreat and be, all sensory, all snowflake, metallic and capable of perceiving the edges of ephemeral dissolve. But out here in the desert, it's a dream, the women swooping eggs from their wombs in charity, to give to me. I am bitter. *Everything melts,* I say, *everything spreads across the surface and fades,* pointing at the mountains above the ocean where a scrubbed pink light makes it hard to breathe, because the color is the smell of the lights gone out, in the linen closet.

Of the baby doll I dragged around in her dirty gown and built a nest for under trees, cloth face and embroidered eyes, I scratched them with my fingernail, "cleaning," the threads so she could see, and fed her stitched half-smile the requisite, miniature bottles of milk and orange juice, the nipples bearing fine white lines, scratched by my teeth.

I didn't, couldn't, imagine any future where I called her in for supper, like my mother leaning out in twilight called my name, into the bluing between stars, hand braced on the knob of the back door, and I came running, hot-cheeked, hair curled in sticks and leaves, the asked for, visibly.

I could see myself taking care of our parakeet until my mother, kneeling at my bedside, said he "croaked" in the night. Such disbelief at a thing, once living, "pretty bird," once preening, while I scraped the peas onto my fork. "Croaked," so we would bury him, in a box of Kleenex behind the shed, his electric green muffled for eternity.

The ground, soaked into my knees, I can't remember if we prayed, and now, past the age my mother was that morning, leading us through trees, I'm still uncertain of what I believe.

I just want a baby, and tired of all the talk, "stop trying and see." In a book I read how the ancients believed birds never died, but rather, passed into the bodies of other birds, which archaeologists say is a belief based on the skeletons, too frail to survive, the pressures of earth.

How to reconcile, when my body absorbs the pressures of earth, the other advice—if I want it—"bad enough" is key, i.e., what message is my body sending, my baby unconceived.

What a womb believes is a stupid riff on the soft-pop song from my childhood: "a fool believes," but "no wise man has the power," of a single grain, in an unlit sea.

To that grain, that seed, that note, that sleep, what shall we call *too much*— the world?

Want is a circle with no relief. So I nurse nothing, unless I nurse myself into silence—

Friends believe you can ask for what it is you would like to receive. These friends have one, or two, or three babies. These friends have learned to whisper around me. They are in accordance with the world, while I traverse its upside-down caverns collecting rocks, shutting everybody but rocks out, giving up the new beliefs, and getting on an old wave with the world, which is more about finding miracles you could never ask for—horse's tooth, pale receipt—and nature, excluding my body.

I pile the rocks in the middle of the kitchen table where Stephen agrees, they help me, despite their frequent nuisance as centerpiece, where flowers, or salt, might go—

I push some of the rocks around while I eat bread and avocado,

one rock from the sea says, to a rock from the desert, "we just disagree," which is another soft song from my childhood, "but don't you see," I write above a drawing of the rocks, "you have come from the same thing, like me—"

and then I get a little literary with my comic, adding the line from Elizabeth Bishop's child self, suddenly terrified about outer-space and all the ways a human body could be. "Why should I be anyone," says the rock, whose eyes I draw aghast, and title this comic, *Even to be a Rock is Hard,* or, *Hope you Find Some Peace.*

In the gold hills scouring rocks, Coda, nursed in my dreams, leans her shiny
panting into my side. On an overhang we sit, my arm around her shoulders,
and we sniff, this particular moment, in pine,

clusters of branched needles arced around our bodies like ladies' fans
dropped, and we have come to the place of after, a calm of fallen things,
that will also one day dissolve.

On the way home, stopped by a bird askew on the dirt, how much time
did she have to get out of one body and into another, born, simultaneously
of air? Can a bird like light quietly continue, or like a scroll of invisible
descendants, keep pumping life into the future,

cell one, cell two, an hour, a billion
in the womb, there's a shadow on the sonogram, like a curtain drawn through

the doctor says, everything appears to be, normal, "though we cannot safely
say what is behind that shadow,

just go on, living."

In the uninsulated house, I reach for fake blue wool and end up in down, thinking about plucked-alive birds whose feathers are "recycled," meaning, their death only happened once, very badly—

I wear the jacket indoors, taking a little for my comfort, so I can go on, able to write about it.

Comfort could be, *birds don't die, only pass into the bodies of other birds,* but what if they weren't finished with their first bodies?

As if to prove how much the sacrifice means, I won't take my jacket off all winter, kneeling in forest, apology split with sun, dear heavenly creatures, I promised not to eat you, yet some of your feathers become me.

This is about trying to recall, a stillness, for instance, what if all the spaces remained spaces, for silence, like cotton pulled, from an empty medicine bottle—

Growing up, we had hundreds of video recordings for dull afternoons,
scrupulously labeled in my father's crimped hand, afraid to forget or lose
anything, meanwhile, the time was always changing, the tapes were out of
date,

        it was the future,
my high shoes, clumping down the wooden stairs to the sounds
of my family,
        fighting, please,
how do we get in and out of, in and out of, where we are supposed to be
inside our bodies, driven by memory,

take our black dog hysterically barking, for hours inside the rotten fence,

take my first time drunk, lying under the dishwasher's open door, "Tiny
Dancer" on stereo, mother out of town, father divorced, screaming at my
friends to *go home,* until I was alone, and turned the volume up to, "it feels
so real," and then, the sickness began

all night, curled on the linoleum, I could sense my world was changing,

in the morning—it was Easter—Jesus rising from the dead to be dead, I knew
I would meet my molester, slipped out, after the dinner, to *see a friend,*
it was a hot day in the abandoned park, I smelled
        of sickness, but wore a '70s style prairie, Salvation Army dress,
that kind of style in my suburban town was the reason boys were not
interested in me, but older men swam toward the alternative, I didn't try, to be,
I thought, if this is as good as it gets, and maybe at least I won't one day have
to, get a job,
        the other future,
        I couldn't imagine, instead, every scenario played I was a
      cashier, with circles under her eyes, and then he put his, fingers,
                inside me,
I just talked to the trees

If I could go back in time and love our old black dog better, even offer her water, then a lot of these memories might not feel so bad. But I could hardly see the animals then, and now, without trying, the icy center of my being has a lot it wishes to atone.

This morning, Coda whimpers at the edge of my sleep, trouble waking in the
dark, reconstructing in hi-def the turning point in my life so far was after

all the parking lots, on the couch, he held his cock in his hands and said,

       "Can I, put this, in you,"

slashing my, favorite season in, two, it was spring, the birds suddenly, a
black parachute, drowning me cacophonous, the cock

       cock pale, there, in the middle of the room

       forever ruined, that little word *put,*
I sank into the cushions, closed my eyes on, the hard silk,

       inside my hand,
turned liquid

Though most of the time, stealth night rides or afternoon excuses, with his hand between my, little house, on the prairie dress, thighs loosed on, the bench seat, or saliva soaking the thin, fabric where my nipples in shadow between, fake pearl before I, turned the corner to return to the, ***what***?

everything's usual

second-hand black lace, like any girl

folding my arms in secret across, the intersection parking lot lunch room

with dyed hair

at home, my mother hung old cartoon bed sheets, in all the downstairs windows, to keep my father from looking in, so all he could see were animal picnics, predominantly bright green, and some rainbows paled by, so much innocent, sleep

At the table, I peeled my orange a day, and photographed a knife about to
fall, which is how I would go to college, not 7-11,

the photograph was called *how I found her in the kitchen later that same year,*
except in the photograph in fact, I am holding the knife, and you can see my
legs in tights, and the fruit is the thing about to fall, the fruit

too soft to eat.

Without his permission suddenly, there was a ripple of summer when I felt good.

The dog, by then, was living with my father, so the house, in between his insistent doorbell, was quiet. Mostly I wanted to disappear, and I thought I could live off this thing I was good at, and taking photographs, the other thing I was good at, and oranges.

I'm still not sure if I convinced myself I was in love, or if I just wanted the hair brushed out of my eyes.

Girls or, whoever, anyone, what would you sacrifice
                to have the hair
brushed out of your eyes?

        First, consider whether your future you,
                will forgive you,

                        or whether,
                like a newborn needs to suck
                        right now, it's non-negotiable,

sometimes, what life is like—to grow up, thinking,
                        this is what life—
                                        is like.

But of that summer's better days, when I could forget need, devouring
Wuthering Heights, a gift from Zach, my best friend who loved boys, with
whom I could almost share my secret, instead I savored that with him, I felt
safe, listening to the Pixies' "Debaser" so loud on his bedroom floor, his
stepfather had to politely knock, uncertain if we were having sex, much to
our hysterical laughter,

and Sundays, skinny-dipped in quarries where we could see our outlines
glow against the massive black rocks below,

> even now, taped to my wall,
> a photograph of Zach, floating like a crucifix of light,

reminds me, of me.

Other trips to the surface, of a world I felt I could participate in, like any cool-kid teenager, pumping two dollars of gas or licking Sweet 'N Low from my palm in the all-night diner, I began to see I had a power, which was, to not need him,

which was to photograph my body naked, but dusted in moldy fruit,

and hung one in the high school gymnasium for a show, algae smudges on my skin, summoned the male principal who didn't know what to say because, I won an award—asked instead was I "ok," and "let this one go," to the pep rally, try to "enjoy your youth,"

snuck out with Zach and Dario, driving through cornfields so fast, windows down for somewhere else.

In college, he kept writing and calling in secret. I could see him pulled over and, quivery, on the side of the road, his hand on his hard cock, hardly able to, breathe, while I just let it, happen to me, eyes on upside-down *Madame Bovary*, 200 pages till morning.

Because I was crazy, still half waiting, I had almost no friends. Lonely a lot, walking through winter trees to eat, alone, but in my college photography class when a girl started documenting ditch-diggers, I realized I could stop taking naked pictures of myself, and instead I took pictures of garbage, or other people, in clothes.

Though the loneliness compelled me to pose for an exchange student who "needed help" on the white paper, studio lighting, so it was he who hung photographs of me, naked, in our class critique. I can't remember what anyone said,

I was completely detached, but now I'd fiercely, like them back.

As a return favor, the exchange student helped me cut my mats, usually a solo activity involving tears, I'd have done anything for help, with the lines.

When I look over that professor's photographs of half-eaten breakfasts and plain-city stores, Midwest windows selling vacuums or shoes, I feel calm inside the green countertops and tumbleweeds, remembering an art that teaches a different kind of desire, and also how he never came on to me,

how he brought his two big dogs to class,

how he said once, about a mat I did cut myself, when pausing to touch its butchered edge, and the whole thing collapsed, onto the floor, that I alone among the students, did not have to redo it, and in that moment, I felt like he saw me

trying to maintain the formal part of living, a frame made with calm measure,

and not to be forever just, the way it *feels,* like the gnashed dirt where I focused my lens, gloveless, in the bitter white of winter, beside the Hudson River.

"All with little veins this morning," the nurse says, binding my arm for blood, I
look at the anesthetic clock, while she inserts, the needle,

the curtain in my womb went away for the picture, so there's space now for
a bird to fly through, in a heavy forest of dusk, dark and light colliding, in a
hollow meant to harbor other bodies, body of my body, of Stephen's body,
or bird, flying, out then in, to whatever we call this, continuation, like a clock
built of breathing,

on the crocheted horse rug intended for the baby, we cannot wear our shoes.
I am trying to preserve it, but Coda always sleeps there, shedding her hair in
the royal blue sky above the horses, and it is just too beautiful to stop,

besides, the last thing I want to do is prevent more living, or prevent living
for the *living*

like a wing, that word

like a bird flies through, so fast, causes bleeding
for the thousandth time pull my finger out of me, note the color and
    the quality,
everything I never learned at 12 or 14, 22 or 33

just stop trying

in my molested days when I smoked weed with his son, I loved him
    because it was true,
"I can't go for you," then years later he died, younger than I am now,
    what life's like,

sometimes hysterical, a high-strung feeling of jangling, need for, release,
slamming the bathroom door until it broke, trapped until the landlord heard
my screaming, had to break down the door, later with ice on my knuckles,
lying in bed, I saw myself in the future, listening to the song, "do you see this
it's rough," I appreciate how she points it out, over and over, "this it's rough,
this it's rough"

Memory is interference from far away, constantly whispered in your ear.

When waking roughly, try to feel the birds, that will one day go on without you, but close enough right now I can see my eyelashes reflected in corners,

a song reached in, black pointed, needles through the blue,

and life follows, on a string attached to, nowhere, so we dedicate ourselves monthly to, trying, to make a baby and the months fall away, like flakes of mica, tiny translucent pages, calendar thinning toward a center we hope has something to reveal,

page without a date, years without a baby, years he touched my body, years of living, in the same body

or are we constantly replaced by, other cells, did he touch, these cells, or which ones, so I can go again and wash them, for the baby.

Remember, little fragments, is how I function, rounding the dirt-packed trail
in the shadow of, indigo mountains I see, a glinting, far-off strip represents
the massiveness, of ocean. I live along the glint like a phrase holds a
paragraph inside it,

sometimes it's all I have to quiet, my anxious mind

but lately I've got a new position in my body, waking to be present,
remember, *Wings of Desire*'s library, of lonely thoughts, all the heads bent
silent, distracted, or deep in texts, when comfort comes under skylights,
spiraling down to touch your sadness, focus on the simple as, hand on hot,
tea in a glass, the moon swallowable as a tablet in dark water,

this morning running from one side of the mountain to the other, not a
soul, but coyotes and me, green stubble through earth and flowered trees,
unraveling.

The doctor points to the largest egg on the sonogram that's about to be released, a glowing orb slightly jostling, like a marble in the pocket of the universe. It's the one that will, possibly, make it, while for now, it's just matter ghostly whistling, without a heart, inside my body,

when something matters it means something.

When I was 16, and my molester fed me for the first time, I felt like this was the path I was meant to go on, but although I took the fruit, I didn't eat. I liked it when my ribs showed, lifting through chemicals, in the darkroom.

Still fight the feeling I was, a seductress, sliding into the lake, in my underwear beneath his, eyes, again embarrassed by the surprise, hadn't planned my, underthings, pattern of pink rosebuds, I swam across the lake, in rosebuds,

while he watched, I floated, for a little while, in the middle feeling the power of the water, around me like a cloak, and not yet climbing out, with wet cloth clinging between my legs but soon, pressed his dry hand, and yes, his tongue then, vividly, in my mouth the water, from my body, streaming,

I felt each of the twisted reeds, beneath my feet, as one thing, as if I could become, *one thing,* not a million particles, clawing

the extent of human, being

while he buried his face, thrashing, into me

Repeatedly trying and failing to conceive, the ghost of my girlhood suspended inside me—many tongues, many fingertips—many failures—whose cause may be the unrelenting question, *am I whole and clear and clean?*

This morning, I drink mint tea with almonds and listen to the freeway. Coda snores on the antique rug, paw covering one eye. I find a picture of him on the internet and he is puffy-faced, perverted. A pale, old pig. And yet his son, who sometimes wrote me emails, is dead.

In one email, the son concluded, "I have been living the dream, as the ditch-diggers say!" I didn't respond directly, for to find out what made life like the dreams of ditch-diggers, was to cross over into vulnerability, a realm I had come to equate with unease.

Perhaps because this son is at peace, I feel freer to speak, to let the lion in the net inside me, exit through my teeth. But even now, a sense of clawing in the chest, when I think of how, surely, he must have a file somewhere with the photographs of me, half naked beside the drawn blinds. A file certainly not labeled *pedophilia,* or *pornography,* and hopefully not, *Meg,* in his mind, in his mouth.

I

MISS

MY

DOLLS

gradually, a tamped down place

In the yellow lamplight
of winter
call it, *threadbare,*
        domesticity,
where lovemaking, or sex,
or fucking would be—where even,
spreading warm hands rivers beneath my shirt—

lie empty—

on the couch the color of freezer packs,

          "BLUE ICE," *no*
          slides into my womb.

The what remains of the bar of soap,
razor thin, incapable of suds:

          this razor jammed inside my sternum.

I touched the pebbled wall, wanted time to feel profound, even ordinary
time to feel, too much, and never stop being, too much, to remember,

I was so young.

I'd been touched by the man for the second time, as he drove me home out
of the forest. A gift-basket of apples spilled, gently bruising under the seat.
Did his wife ever know he drove one-handed with me

Take everything about babies
out. Mothering,
out, milk,
night waking,
rocking, sucking, *ooooh,*
      there there,
satisfied?

I miss my dolls. Packed in collapsing boxes in my father's attic, and closed in drawers with flowery handles, beside the bed where I learned how to bawl. The theatrics of suffocation in disheveled sheets. Some of the dolls, their faces wrapped in paper towels. Some of the dolls, their heads falling off. Some with insects' lacework across the aprons, or holes in their hollow torsos, limbs carried off by the dog. I used to pull a doll's puffy undergarments down and feel disappointed, or perhaps, confused, to see only smooth. I used to shove a doll's hips back into her semi-circle stand, after bending her at the waist, or toying with her hair: the equivalent of play, for dolls on display. For years, they lined the heart-shaped shelves in my room. Gradually, dust, like tiny gray curls, pearled in each outfits' folds. Long lashed, bud-mouthed, petite, and dumb, every one. I began to feel it—had had enough of their childishness, and packed them away—not long before I was touched by the man three times my age. Not long before my body on the bench seat shook; before, in forest dark, my body burned. Then it went into a box, too.

Thought I needed to protect the innocent, and therefore, could only speak obscurely, through objects typically viewed as garbage. Messages were encoded in plucked from the ground, fragments that I could tape to the wall, or line on a windowsill to love. Watches, doll shoes, animal bones. The wayward scribble. My gathering made meaning like God gives. It could be called *art* or *diary* or *evidence—trying how to live.*

Robin said, "Trauma reiterates." In each telling, the facts: first, *I was sad,* then, *I was molested,* and therefore, *I fell in love with the trash.*

[insert garbage poem]

Kleenex, particle,
baby,

ink pours out of my mouth

(crooked glasses in the dogshit grass
valentine, gum wrapper, Big Gulp)

Black-out things come back to me:

in a sundress, it was summer.
I was the wedding photographer
for his dead son.

Of what's missing, I do not need a reminder,
nor the sage-old advice to meditate,
empty my brain, love
what is absent and cold.
What's bleak is snow.
What's bleak is *no.*
The womb almost on empty,
like the gas tank running low.
We left the ocean for the farmland
to buy a house for a baby,
but the baby never arrives.
Forget the tiny socks in a grocery sack.
Forget the circadian blue skies.
To cope, I thought we'd get a couple of goats—
the kind that are small enough
to carry—the kind that never cry.

A specific place on the wall, to touch, moving my finger just above the wall, to touch, dirty white paint, *Will you remember this moment in which nothing, happens for the rest of your life? (First, try to remember this moment, in which nothing—*

I'd like a print of every sonogram I ever had, to present, like mothers do, on the refrigerator, or untuck from my wallet relentlessly. Anyone would strain to see life in the black waves. *Just keep looking,* I'd say. Echo in the body, one beat. Dumb of my womb, lit stars. As a teenager, the constant fear of pregnancy:

> *can I,*
> *put this,*
> *in you?*

terror of my belly
mounding,
stood sideways in mirrors, examined
obsessively, sharp-eyed
       at any reflection, for something more

that every pinch
was a fingernail formed inside me,
a small tail,

> a hiccup I banished with wishing,
> that little word *put*—

> I want to end on a different kind of no.

my own, i.e.

When I ask my father to photograph my dolls, he drapes my stuffed worm over the brass knob of the screen door. The door has not begun to rot. The worm wears a green beret. Through the screen you can see down the hall, into the kitchen and out the window to the backyard, where dusk clouds a pollened gold. There, I sucked my cheeks and swung. Forsythia fighting perimeter. The noise of insects overtaking.

When I tried to hold the stuffed stick of its body, I came up with myself.

Fifty-billion glassy blinks

    called dreaming or *ago.*

How harmless, the newly cut grass, flotsam of its former living.

ACKNOWLEDGEMENTS

The poem beginning "I was so young" first appeared in *The Times Literary Supplement* in a slightly different form and "Garbage Miracles" first appeared in *Ninth Letter*. I am grateful to these publications for featuring my work. The epigraph by Dennis Silk is quoted in the book *On Dolls* edited by Kenneth Gross. "Are you entering the room nobody knows" is a line written to me by my dear friend, Jim Lingo. The phrase "satin rafters" is a nod to Emily Dickinson's poem, "Safe in their Alabaster Chambers—." I also reference Dickinson's "Banish Air from Air—" and her letter to Mary Bowles ("The Heart wants what it wants—"). "Everything that does not need you is real" is borrowed from W.S. Merwin's poem the "The Widow." Further, I am indebted to Daneen Wardrop's *Emily Dickinson and the Labor of Clothing* for her historical research on fabric, which informed the poem on page 39.

The dental floss sculpture referenced is by my collaborator and dear friend, Jamie Boyle. "What aches to look at," was written to me by another dear friend and mentor, Ann Hamilton. The "pen and ink mouth" image is inspired by a scene from *Belladonna of Sadness*, illustrated by Kuni Fukai and directed by Eiichi Yamamoto. The Kate Bush song I obsessively listened to in high school, referenced here as Bush, "braying like a donkey," comes from the song, "Get out of My House," from her album, *The Dreaming*. The soft pop songs I reference are "What a Fool Believes" by The Doobie Brothers and "We Just Disagree" by Dave Mason. The line by Elizabeth Bishop reads in full, "Why should I be my aunt, / or me, or anyone," and is from her poem, "In the Waiting Room," which I have long carried with me. The Walt Whitman quote is from *Leaves of Grass*. All bird book allusions are thanks in part to Branka Arsić's *Bird Relics: Grief and Vitalism in Thoreau*. "Tiny Dancer" is a song by Elton John. Stephen Shore is the artist whose photographs I allude to. "Do you see this it's rough" is a line by Merce Lemon, from her beautiful album, *Ideal for a Light Flow with Your Body*. *Wings of Desire* is a film by Wim Wenders. The idea that, "trauma reiterates" comes from my dear friend and poet, Robin Clarke. Finally, some of the dolls, particularly those in, "I Miss My Dolls," are designed by Madame Alexander, and are intended for collection, not play.

I am beyond grateful for the wisdom and support of so many people, without whom this book could not have been written. Thank you especially to Natalie Shapero for your friendship and insight throughout. Thank you to Solmaz Sharif for helping me see the whole of the manuscript and for challenging me with the last difficult questions to bring it into form. Thank you to Jamie Boyle, Emily Carlson, Robin Clarke, Elizabeth Gramm, and Christine Poreba for your crucial support and feedback at various points in the writing. Thank you to Ann Hamilton for the long and beautiful back-and-forth. Thank you to Zachary Holbrook for the best hard laughs that truly keep me going. Thank you to Ann Carlson, Sten Carlson, Olivia Ciummo, Ricky Crano, Cory Dallas, Dina Dean, Sally Glatfelter, Kevin A. González, Mary Haberle, Amber Hall, Hilary Hopkins, Richard Kraft, Jim Lingo, Calista Lyon, Thom McCaffrey, Marie Tae McDermott, Alison McNulty, Adele Mattern, Jessica Murray, Andrew Nease, Rachel Nelson, Lisa Pearson, Cormac Slevin, and Joshua Zelesnick for your friendship and art. Thank you to the 2019 Tin House Winter Poetry Workshop, particularly Jessica Abughattas, Joshua Burton, Alonso Llerena, Caitlin Roach, and Michelle Phương Ting, all of whom offered invaluable feedback and encouragement in the final stages.

Thank you to Deborah Burnham and the Pennsylvania Governor's School for the Arts for the early connections in my life between people and poetry that never stop giving. Thank you to my teachers and classmates at Sarah Lawrence College, Bard College, University of Florida, and The Ohio State University. Thank you to Stephen Shore. Thank you to my acupuncturist, Michael Niss, for your healing. Thank you to my parents, Linda Spiece Burgoon and Edward Shevenock, Jr., for letting me quit sports to write poetry, and for believing that I could. Thank you to Bob Hicok for selecting my manuscript, and to William Waltz, Scott Bruno, and the amazing team at Conduit Books for putting it into the world: it's an honor to work with you.

Thank you to the mountain light of Los Angeles, and all the animals, plants, and birds I ran among in the early mornings, before coming home awakened, to write this book. And thank you to my partner Stephen, for your daily love and encouragement, and to our Coda, the miraculous always.

ABOUT THE AUTHOR

Meg Shevenock has worked with gifted students through an approach of associative learning for the past eleven years. More recently, she has been the "reader" for the artist Ann Hamilton. Meg's poems and essays have appeared in *The Times Literary Supplement, Lana Turner, Best New Poets, Denver Quarterly, Ninth Letter, Prairie Schooner, 32 Poems, jubilat, Kenyon Review* blog, and elsewhere. She maintains an ongoing telepathic art practice with her collaborator Jamie Boyle. Meg lives in Columbus, Ohio.

CONDUIT BOOKS
& EPHEMERA

OTHER TITLES FROM CONDUIT BOOKS & EPHEMERA

Sacrificial Metal by Esther Lee

Animul/Flame by Michelle Lewis

The Last Note Becomes Its Listener by Jeffrey Morgan